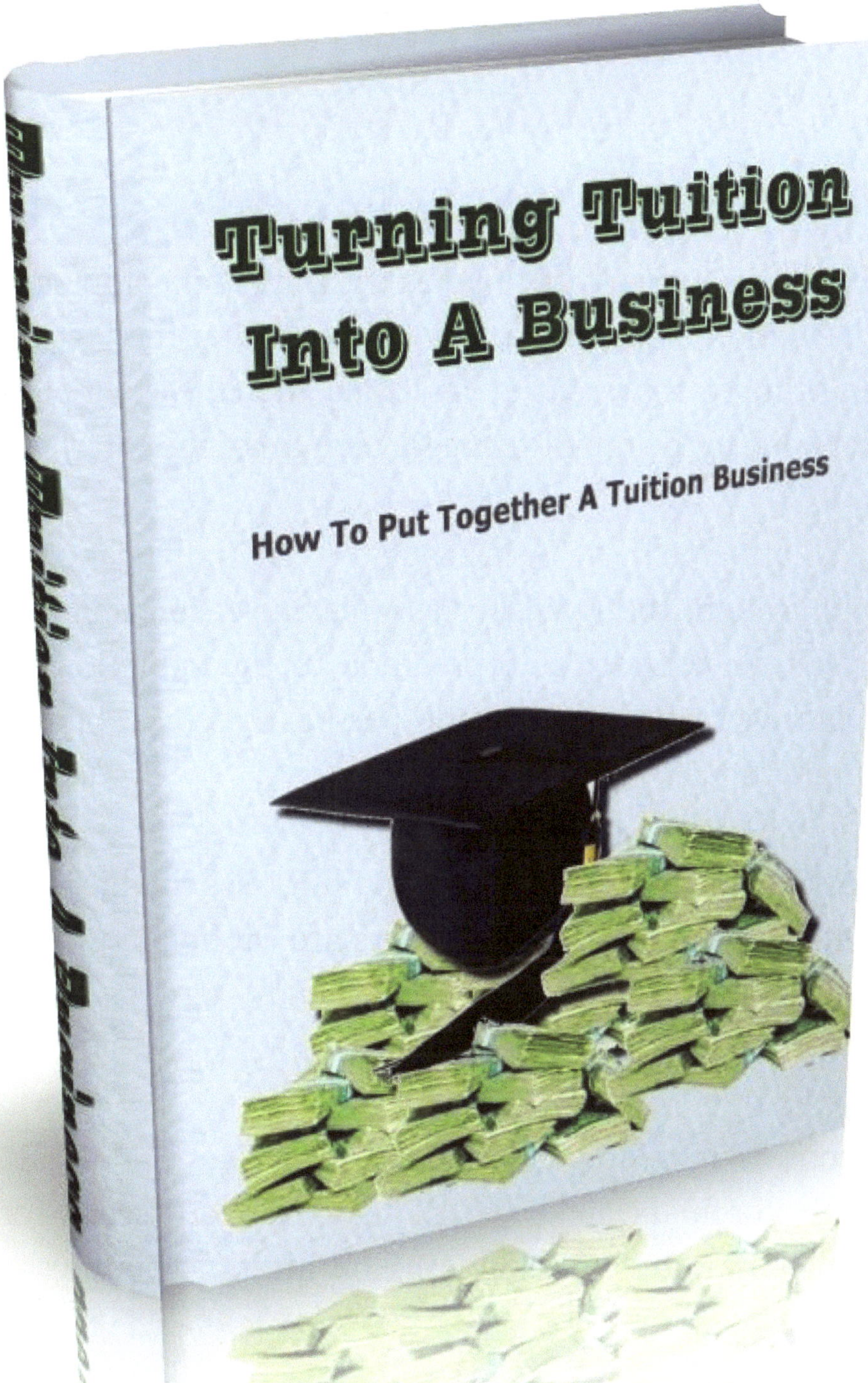

Turning Tuition Into A Business

How To Put Together A Tuition Business

Terms and Conditions

Table Of Contents

Foreword

As with all business endeavors, there is a need to do some research into the intended field before actually making the commitment to start the business entity. Several different factors should be carefully considered and weighed, in order to ensure the right decisions are made. Get all the info you need here.

Turning Tuition Into A Business
How To Put Together A Tuition Business

Chapter 1:
Tuition Business Basics

Synopsis

The following are some guidelines and recommendations of the areas that need attention during the research phase of the exercise:

The Basics

There is a need to identify the niche or void the intended business is capable of filling. If this identification process proves to be fruitful there is a better chance of venturing into a field that will yield positive results.

However if this is not identified there is also the real possibility of venturing into an already saturated market thus creating unwanted competition and stress for the new business owner.

Once the niche market has been identified, the next step would be to discern the type of services intended to be extended to serve this niche market.

As in the case of the tutorial style of business, thought must be given to the actual topics or subjects that are intended to be offered as part of the services.

Once this has been decided, the business owner must ensure the relevant assisting tools and manpower is available to fill this service being offered.

Although by this point the element of relevance would and should already been taken into consideration, however the point should be revisited to ensure the actual revenue earning possibilities and projections have been weighted against the infrastructure that is now identified and in place.

Lastly there should be some search done on the nearest competition of the business and how the said competition is functioning at the present moment.

If the existing market available is already quite small it would not be wise to enter into this kind of business as there would be the constant pressure to "fight" for the market share.

Chapter 2:

Why Start A Tuition Business

Synopsis

There are many reasons why people make the decision to start up their own business ventures. Some of these reasons may include the need for another source of income, a need work for one's self, a need for more flexible work time frames and many others.

Any one of these reasons can be attributed to the interest in wanting to venture into the tuition business. However one should consider deeply the reason for the desire to start up this particular business venture.

How Come

The following are some reasons given as to why there may be an interest in starting up a tuition business:

Besides the obvious affinity the individual must have towards the educational expansion of young minds, there is also the probability of the business owner starting such a venture for the simple need of wanting to be the "boss".

Having a love for the education field will prompt the individual into venturing further and turning the love into a business. The idea of packaging and selling a particular style of education that is quite individualistic, maybe something the new business owner is interested in focusing upon.

Being able to promote something that is designed and marketed based on a personal style or dream can be a very powerful tool to tap into when venturing into business.

If the research done indicated a very high percentage of revenue earning possibilities, then tuition style business venture could prove to be not only mentally rewarding but also financially so.

If the individual and the team that has been identified to be part of the tutorial business are both experienced and accomplished then the revenue earning possibility is heightened further based on the projected popularity of the teaching tools and staff intended.

Starting a tuition business, also allows the individual to be able to reach out to others on an educational platform, where his or her personal style is given a level of freedom that is less likely to be restricted.

Chapter 3:

Arranging Your Business

Synopsis

Once the individual has identified the need to venture into the tuition business, preferably after all the relevant research supporting this decision has been carried out, the next step would be to actually get into the actual motions of setting up the venture.

Putting It Together

There are several smaller though equally significant areas that should be looked into during the setting up process and the following points will help to highlight these areas:

After identifying the specific type of tuition business the owner has decided to venture into, the location that would be ideal for the particular niche identified should be sought.

The location for the intended tuition business venture is pivotal to the success of the business. There must be an already existing and available market to tap into around the intended location.

Once the location has been identified all the relevant legal documents and licenses have to be filed and the relevant authorities contacted for such purposes.

Only when approval of the business venture has been given and the venture legalized, then the other follow up steps can be taken.

These steps would include the actual purchasing of the equipment and tools for the tuition venture set up. The teaching staff needs to be hired and the renovations, if needed should commence.

Other elements such as advertising props and such should also be designed and posted wherever necessary to attract the attention of the general public and the targeted customer base.

Launch dates for the opening should be advertised prominently along with any "early bird" promotions to create the excitement and interest to sign up and be part of the tuition system.

If the advertising campaign is well planned and executed, there should ideally be a good response to the tuition business, thus managing to garner the desired revenue projected.

Chapter 4:

Running A Successful Tuition Business

Synopsis

Running a successful tuition business does not require a huge capital or any other kind of investment other than time and dedication. Teaching is a rewarding line to get into if there is a natural love for the imparting of education unto young minds.

Success

The following are some recommendation that should be considered if a new business owner intends to make a success of the tuition business venture:

Being able to give close and personal attention to each student is a very attractive feature to incorporate into the design and structure of each tutorial session.

People often chose to attend such tuition centers for the specific reason of being able to get this more focused attention which cannot be gotten through the more conventional schooling system.

Introducing periodical consultation sessions with parents of participating students is another highly valued service. This will enable all parties to be informed and all grievances to be addressed before any dissatisfaction sets in.

The extended service of providing extra classes when and if needed, is also another attractive service to include. This would be especially beneficial around exam time where both parents and student alike would certainly appreciate the added attention and guidance.

Making the effort to provide a specially designed environment that looks and feels professional will also be advantages towards setting the standards to be expected at the establishment.

However in doing so there should also be some effects put in to encourage the calm and study friendly atmosphere that would encourage student to be comfortable and alert.

A team of professionals, who are dedicated and keen to impart their knowledge in a friendly and accommodating manner, should be a prerequisite and apparent.

Most students are looking for help when they seek out the services of a tuition centre, therefore a teaching staff that is both approachable and dedicated will ensure the popularity of the establishment.

Chapter 5:

Advertizing Your Tuition Business

Synopsis

Being in the tutoring business can be very rewarding both monetarily as well as mentally. Being b able to impart knowledge to excited young minds is an exhilarating experience and well worth the effort when those young minds become formidable personalities of the future.

Ads

The following are some tips on how to go about advertising the tuition business endeavor:

Creating some level of visibility toward the target audience intended is one of the first challenges to commit to. Depending on the demographic the style of advertising will vary quite a bit.

However starting out with simple flyers and business cards should create the interest in the tutoring establishment. When designing the business card one should ideally include all teaching credential to assure potential clients that the tuition center is built of solid foundations in education.

Attending school functions and parent teacher meetings with the intention of introducing the tuition business to the ideal group of potential customers.

Posting the advertisement in areas frequented by potential clients will help to gain their attention without having to spend on lavish advertising campaigns.

These popular places may include bulletin boards, coffee shops, supermarkets, and stored. Visiting local schools and making presentation on the merits of signing up at the tuition centre is also another way to create visibility for the centre.

However the presentation should be designed to be impactful and convincing in promoting the tuition centre.

Advertising online using the various complimenting tools is also something worth looking into. This is especially advantageous when some of these tools are considerably cheaper or even free.

Advertising free trial sessions is also fast gaining popularity as the students and parents who are concerned with the standard to the establishment can get firsthand experience and feel of the place. Most times when people are made welcome and the environment is suitable getting them to sign on is usually not a huge problem.

Chapter 6:

The Benefits Of running A Tuition Business

Synopsis

The following are some benefits to be derived from running a tuition business:

Advantages

Venturing into one's own business provides the opportunity to be the "boss" and this then presents the privacy platform to exercise personal judgment and business acquirement.

The need to share authority and get consent for everything is not longer applicable when one has his or her own business and this freedom can be exhilarating and enticing.

The tuition business is something that is looked upon with a certain amount of respectability, as this esteemed profession is normally built around people with integrity and commitment to the nurturing of young minds.

Therefore being a part of this profession will give the individual a sense of giving back to society in a way that is gratifying both mentally and monetarily.

Having the luxury of working at one's own dictated pace is the desire of most working adults and through the tuition business platform such a scenario can be effectively achieved.

This also presents another advantage of being able to spend or a lot more time for personal relationships, family and friends. Being is a regular work frame does not allow such breaks to be taken in order to spend quality time whenever and wherever the need arises, thus the reason why some people are opting to have their own businesses.

Of course another dominant factor and attraction in the income earning possibilities that are evident with this type of venture. With comparatively low financial commitment expectations, the possibilities of earning high revenue is indeed almost limitless.

Wrapping Up

There are many reasons an individual would be interested in starting a tuition business. However before one does decide to venture into this field all the relevant researches should be done to ensure this particular style is suitable for the individual.